Bitcoin Trading and Investing:

A Complete Beginners Guide to Buying, Selling, Investing and Trading Bitcoins

BENJAMIN TIDEAS

ISBN: 1511757809
ISBN-13: 9781511757805

CONTENTS

INTRODUCTION

I want to congratulate you and thank you for picking up this book, "Bitcoin Trading and Investing: A Complete Beginners Guide to Buying, Selling, Investing and Trading Bitcoins".

The digital rush sweeping the globe, and, in particular, the internet, has centered around investors of all ages and lifestyles cashing in on Bitcoin. It's the infamously unpredictable cryptocurrency that makes trading and investing as easy as sitting in front of your laptop. However, what is easy is not always simple. Part of the reason it is difficult to grasp is because it has not been around for long – there is no way to truthfully psychoanalyze the comings and goings, the rises and the falls of what your currency can do. Getting involved with Bitcoin is easier and riskier than the traditional ways we think about investitures. However, just like with Wall Street, there are ways to become more proficient in the art of trading and investing.

As with any exchange, market, or online platform that requires a credit card, trading with Bitcoin is risky to those who are new, and those who have been working at it for quite some time. Though you probably will never hold Bitcoins in your hands, it can hurt your bottom line – you might lose real money. The most important advice you can receive is to proceed with caution and make sure you are not pushing yourself deep into a hole.

This book will try to educate you on the options you have when it comes to trading and investing with Bitcoin. Read thoroughly before you try to start the process, make notes, and maybe sit by a prospect what is going on before you venture out on your own.

Thanks again for grabbing this book, I hope you enjoy it!

Also, Don't forget to grab your FREE Bonus book via the link at the end!

Now, let's get started!

REAL LIFE USAGE

With the emergence of Bitcoins as a major currency, there has been a need to use them in daily life, not just on the computer. While this is still emerging technology, there are a few ways to use Bitcoins to make purchases at stores, online, and for events.

Bitcoin ATMS

A Bitcoin ATM is an electronic communications device that allows a person to exchange bitcoins for cash without being connected to the internet or his or her wallet. There are two chief types of Bitcoin ATMs available in certain sections of the population. The basic units, which are more prevalent, allow the customer to only buy Bitcoins. The more complex machines, which are emerging but not as prevalent, will let a person buy as well as sell bitcoins via the machine. It's a completely revolutionary way for people to stay on top of their trading while they are on vacation, on business, or just away from computer access. There is one catch, however. In order to be able to access the more advanced and premium features of the complex units, you will usually need to be a member of the ATM manufacturer that operates the machine.

The first Bitcoin ATM was a Robocoin in a coffee shop in Canada. Soon the United States caught on. Most Bitcoin ATMS are located inside of independently owned coffee shops. There are currently 285 Bitcoin ATM Machines installed worldwide, but that number is always fluctuating.

In order to find a Bitcoin ATM, users can check the following websites:

- CoinATMRadar.com

- BitcoinATMmap.com
- Bitcoin ATM Locator by Forexmex.com

There is one problem: the more Bitcoin ATMs there are, the more, it seems hackers seem to target them.

Retailers Accepting Bitcoins

There are many different websites and retailers that accept Bitcoins as payment. Some even offer specials or discounts to those who use them. Here are some as of this writing:

- Microsoft – use on Windows, Windows phones, and Xbox
- Dell – Accepts Bitcoin through a partnership with Coinbase. Sometimes there are specials for users. Dell is the biggest acceptor of Bitcoins.
- Overstock – One of the first major retailers to accept the currency. Bitcoin purchases are open to over 100 countries.
- Newegg – A retail giant based in Los Angeles-based company. It specializes in computer hardware and software, but also sells a variety of appliances and goods.
- Show Room Prive – The largest European Company to accept the payment via the company Paymium. Is not valid on the mobile platform.
- TigerDirect - the online retailer of computers and consumer electronics now accepts payments in Bitcoin,
- Bitcoinshop.us - Offers products from air-conditioners to watches, all priced in Bitcoin for those wanting to make a purchase. The catch: it only ships to people in the continental US.
- BitcoinStore.com - Sells electronics and ships worldwide, but shipping rates vary.

The good news for those who don't like to make purchases on the internet is that there are hundreds of small retailers accepting bitcoin too. Coinmap, Spendbitcoins.com, and UseBitcoins.info keep up-to-date databases of these shopping destinations.

HOW BITCOIN WORKS

Though we've gone further in depth with this in a previous book, let us first start with a brief description of what Bitcoin is, and how it functions as a currency. The first step in trading Bitcoins is really understanding what they are, where they come from, and how to acquire more. Bitcoin is just like any other form of money though it is digital. As with other real forms of money, it can be saved, spent, invested, and even stolen through no fault of your own. What began as a small online forum in 2009 by someone using the name Satoshi Nakamoto, has grown in value and prestige in just a few short years. The value of the "dollar" or coin has also jumped significantly.

One generates Bitcoins through a process called "mining." Without going into too much detail, this is essentially using your computer's processor to solve complex algorithms known as "blocks." You will earn about fifty Bitcoins per block of you have decrypted. There is a fairly large catch, depending on your computer and CPU, solving a single block can take you over a year. Another way to put Bitcoins into your virtual wallet is to simply purchase them using another form of money – you exchange it at a Bitcoin exchange station like Mt. Gox or Bitstamp. There are many services all over the internet and they pop up randomly all of the time. The most important thing to do is make sure are reputable and trustworthy. Make sure you read testimonials and ensure that the website is not going to take your money.

EXCHANGES

Bitcoin exchanges happen just like physical currency exchanges do: you are purchasing one form of currency and trading it with another.

The relative value of whatever nation you are in is a reflection of the country's economy, financial health, and world status. For example, the U.S. dollar is worth more than that of the Mexican peso at the current time because of the differences between the economies. These values constantly fluctuate. The same type of thing happens with Bitcoins. The relative value is determined by the worked performed by your individual computer. This also opens up a pathway that allows Bitcoins to be traded like commodities – just the way we trade eggs, playing cards, and secrets.

You make physical money by using those previously mentioned websites as an intermediary for transactions between Bitcoins and national currencies. You watch the unpredictable shifts in relative values and simply trade back and forth. That's how some people make money – they simply shift money around when it is the proper moment. This is known as arbitrage, and it is probably the simplest form of trading available to Bitcoin users: but that also means many more people will lose money trying to navigate the twists and turns.

HOW TO BECOME A PLAYER IN THE BITCOIN MARKET

Knowing the risks and rewards, one can venture toward trading and invest in Bitcoins. There are quite a few different ways to go about making money for your trades. The best approach is to come up with a lump sum to keep yourself in line. You don't want to get too obsessed with "playing the market" or watching the rises and falls of the value.

Bitcoins are stored in a digital wallet that exists on your computer. Do not store large amounts of money in your Bitcoin wallet. Instead, keep them stored offline or in something known as "cold storage." Remember to keep your identity hidden when you are making a transaction. Your comings and goings will be registered in a public log – but the buyer and seller of the goods are not revealed.

BECOMING A BITCOIN TRADER

There are several ways to dip your toes into the Bitcoin market and become a trader. Anyone can do it, and each entry point ranges from simple to difficult. Let's introduce a few of the ways to get wet in the Bitcoin trading market.

Bitcoin Mining

Mining is the easiest and slowest way into the market. Your best bet is to get a computer that will do nothing but mine for Bitcoins. You will have to install some software and just completely let the computer go – anything else you do is just causing you to lose money. It is best to build your own computer that works extremely fast - some computers can take upwards of a year to actually see any profits. For this reason, mining has become a second thought to anyone who isn't sporting a full server center (yes, hundreds of boxes) with the newest, most powerful ASIC machines.

Mining Bitcoins is at a stage now where you probably won't make back your investment any time soon, if you actually ever do. In truth, you are far more likely to see a greater profit margin if you go out and sell lemonade at the local pool during the summer. There are a few different things you can do, however, to make earning more Bitcoins easier and faster.

Trading Bots

Mt. Gox was one of the first to develop an automated trading bot, dubbed "Willy" to do some of the work for you. These bots, which aren't universally loved, trade on the financial markets so that users don't miss out on any potential sales. The question is – what exactly are these bots and can they really make money for you?

Trading bots are not humans, but are actually software programs that interact directly to the financial exchanges, and place buy and sell orders on your behalf using artificial intelligence and algorithms. They make those decisions by watching the market's price movements and reacting according to a set of predefined rules. They aren't as good as humans are, of course, but they can let you sleep soundly.

Examples of other types of bots include the Butter Bot, which even features an online trading bot accessed via a Google Chrome plug-in, and Haas Online, which sells a Windows-based personal trading server. Another, Crypto Trader offers a trading bot marketplace, which allows people to develop bots using different trading strategies, and then rent them to others. This is the best chance to personalize a bot and make it work just like you would. Still, that takes a lot of effort and know-how.

Trading by algorithm isn't new in the financial world or even gambling, in general: companies in the conventional financial markets have been using the method for years. This empowers individual traders to have their computer access the exchange's electronic order books directly. That's a service normally only available to brokers and investment houses in the conventional markets. Once again, this isn't something that will take away the work for you, but will supplement what you already do. Pablo Lema, the founder of Butter Bot, says that bots aren't a 'fire and forget' technology that enable dilettantes to make money without trying:

"Trading bots require users to have at least a basic understanding of the market, need to be modified and tweaked by the user according to the predominant market conditions, and also according to their own risk profile."

Trading Bot Strategy

But of course you know that trading isn't necessarily based on technical analysis and algorithms alone. It's difficult to program a computer to react to fundamental market conditions such as, say, rumors about the market shut down or an upcoming news piece that will cause money to flood the market.

Many bots will use an exponential moving average (EMA) as a starting point. These averages act to track market prices over an established time span, and bots can be programmed to react to what that price does – such as moving beyond certain thresholds.

It's Not for Everyone

Is bot trading the solution for you? Possibly, but not definitely. They do offer a variety of rewards, not least of which is the ability to diligently trade on your behalf, 24/7, and the ability to remove all of the emotions from trading. Plus they allow you to "live and let live" – some people, especially newer traders, are too antsy with the clicking and make mistakes.

On the other hand, if you don't have the financial know-how to put together a trading strategy that will work for you and your bot, you could simply end up automating a set of poor market trading decisions.

Once again, whether or not you decide to automate your trades, the basic rules apply: don't trade more than you can afford to lose, and don't go into any investment without at least a basic understanding of what you're doing.

Finally, do yourself a favor and get a true assessment of what your risk tolerance really is. Many people think their tolerance is very high, but when they lose a large sum due to a market turn, they find quite abruptly that this is not so. Go here to find yours: Investment Risk Tolerance Quiz

Create a Gang

A "gang" or mining pool is an option. To use a mining pool, you have to find people to connect computers with so that you can all work together to break up the block. The money that comes from that block is then shared amongst the owners of the computers. However, it all depends on how much work your individual computer has put out – you won't get coins for just connecting and not putting in the work.

You can find pools all over the internet, just a simple Google search will amass millions of results. Bitcoin also has a large list of these popular mining gangs that you can join. The gangs from Bitcoin will give you a lot more information as to the team makeup, including where certain fees will go.

However, the level of security, if it is used at all, deviates from mining pool to mining pool. Some pools require only a Bitcoin trading username while others require the traditional two-step Google authentication process. Still, Bitcoin remains as anonymous as ever, and you won't have to give out any personal information or numbers. This is a positive, as you are sometimes dealing with substantial amounts of money and sensitive information.

Head Straight for the Markets

Another approach you can take though it is by far the riskiest move of all, is to jump right into the market and get to work. All you have to do is sign up with one of the companies listed above (Mt. Gox being the largest, oldest, and most profitable). Give them your email address, create a username, and confirm your account. It's fairly easy!

After you have confirmed your account, the website you chose will ask you to provide some forms that prove your identity, location, and tax status. These forms will most likely include any of the following:

- Any document issued by the or county, city, or the federal government;
- State of Residence Vehicle Registration Card or title;
- State of Residence Voter Precinct Card;
- Military Orders/Documents;
- Utility bill or cable bill;
- Housing lease or contract, mortgage statement, property or income tax statement;
- Preprinted financial statement;
- School records;
- State of Residence Vehicle insurance policy;
- Letter from the homeless shelter

You will also have to provide some form of identification that shows you have proof of a legal presence within the United States or country of your choice. These documents include:

- I-551 Permanent Resident Card
- Machine Readable Immigrant Visa
- I-766 Employment Authorization Card
- Temporary I-551 stamp on I-94 or Passport
- I-327 Re-entry Permit with supporting immigration documentation
- I-94 Arrival/Departure Record
- I-20 accompanied by I-94
- DS-2019 accompanied by I-94

- I-571 Refugee Travel Document with supporting immigration documentation
- I-797 Notice of Action
- I-521L Authorization for Parole of an Alien into U.S. with supporting immigration documentation
- I-220B Order of supervision with supporting immigration documentation

Some web sites, though not all, will ask for proof for Social Security purposes. You will need to provide at least one of these documents:

- Social Security Card
- 1099 Tax Form
- W-2 Form
- DD-214 Form
- Payroll Record
- Social Security Document reflecting the Social Security Number
- Military Record reflecting the Social Security Number
- Medicaid/Medicare Card reflecting the Social Security Number

Most of these documents are things you'll have sitting around the house if you need them, so they shouldn't be too difficult to get. However, you will need to scan the documents in and send them to the company before you can start.

After you go through all of that, it is simply a matter of putting what you made into your account and watching the market on a daily or hourly basis for the opportunity to buy and sell to make more money. Some exchanges will charge a fee on any transaction you make, which will range from .25 per trade to .60 per trade. This is how these companies make money – because people know has the chance to be the most successful venture for them.

Playing the markets requires you to be alert. You do stand a chance to lose some of your money through this method. In fact, it is probably the riskier option overall. You should only choose this method if you are willing to dedicate a large chunk of your time to this process. You can't only check the numbers once a week. Those who make the most money constantly pay attention to the rises and falls, and sell as soon as they know the time is right. If you don't have the time because you are working a lot or raising a family, you should consider another approach like a mining pool or mining by yourself.

Whichever way you choose to go: mining, joining a gang, or playing the market by yourself, there are risks and rewards associated with all of them. It really depends on what you want to get out of the entire process.

Mining takes longer, might not get you a profit, but is solitary and doesn't require you to work with people or constantly pay attention. However, it is very solitary and won't get you a lot of money.

Joining a mining pool is a somewhat more social experiment, but requires you to be at the mercy of other people and their computers, something that scares people away from doing that particular way of trading and making money.

Playing the market is the way to go for someone who wants to see instant action or results. However, it isn't for people who don't have income to lose. You will probably make mistakes for the first few months that you try to work with the market, and will keep doing so until you get a proper read for it.

RISKS AND REWARDS

Now that you know how to start your way into Bitcoin trading and investing, you should probably know the risks in detail. It's one thing to hear about the categories, but you also need to know what you are setting yourself up for. Most of these aren't problems, they are just things that will take you a little more time when you do your taxes or balance your checking account. Still, there are some risks and rewards you need to know about.

The Volatility of the Market

For most other forms of trading, including the stock market, the value of the currency rises and falls in a predictable way at a predictable speed. Rarely are there intense crashes in value or surges in costs. However, that is not the case with Bitcoin. The value of the Bitcoin falls and soars radically throughout the day, sometimes peaking the morning or peaking at night – there is rarely a rhyme or reason for it to happen. It can leap dollars in an instance, or tumble at the same speed. This means that if you do not have your nose to the grindstone constantly, you will be at risk of losing large amounts of money.

To stay on top and avoid feeling the sting of the volatility, you can join newsgroups on social media, download apps, and make friends within the game that will keep you alerted of the comings and goings. All it takes is one country to ban cryptocurrency, and the whole thing will collapse, losing all of your money in its path. For example, 36 hours after China imposed a ban on cryptocurrency, 75% of users saw dramatic reductions in their money. Keeping abreast of the news will allow you to make decisions after thinking about them, instead of making rash decisions when an event happens or directly after.

You want people to hold onto their digital commodities, however. That is how the market stabilizes. Be careful when you make friends that you aren't getting tricked by someone who is only looking out for himself or herself. Some people like to do the "sit and wait" game, and that has made some people quite a bit of money. However, many others get a thrill off of short selling or playing the market and making handfuls of money that way. It's all up to you and the way the market decides to shift.

Paying Taxes on Bitcoin Income

Bitcoins do come with tax implications and can be taxed by the federal, state, and local governments. There is a tax when you cash out your Bitcoins with any banking firm, or when you show dividends at the end of the year. Bitcoin is what many tax specialists would call an "asset." When you without any of your income from Bitcoin, you are actually committing a federal crime. Think of it are a bartering system, your Bitcoins are your goods, but they still have a monetary value that one cannot simply ignore.

It is best not to do your own taxes if you are frequently working with Bitcoins or you are working with a large amount of money. Do some searching online and find someone who specializes in working with Bitcoin operations. More and more tax firms are bringing in people who can help with that process so that you don't accidentally cause any problems between you and the state or you and the feds.

Getting Attacked by a Cyber Criminal

You probably are not the only person who finds the rise of the Bitcoin as something you can use to get yourself some money. The dramatic and highly publicized rise in the value of the Bitcoin has caught the attention of many cyber criminals. Why? There is an extremely low risk of getting caught. If you are not constantly vigilant and you make a bit of money, you will be at risk for hackers.

For example, one marketplace called The Sheep Marketplace had a totally of 96,000 Bitcoins that were worth nearly $220 million US dollars – quite a bit of change. In early 2013, all of that was stolen. Similarly, some cyber criminals attack smaller scale accounts because they are typically easier to hack and add up over time.

Criminals will most likely try targeting computers connected to the internet without a good firewall, and break into the wallets. They use phishing tactics, malware, social engineering, and other malicious tasks that will create quite a mess for you to clean up. In November of 2012, thieves stole a million dollars' worth of Bitcoins from a Denmark-based payment processor. The result was a lot of lost money and headaches for everyone involved.

But don't think those cyber hackers cannot get to you if they can't get to your account. That particular attack made the Bitcoin prices drop dramatically from 49.10 dollar all the way to 39.30 dollars in a matter of nine short hours. This happened because there was a fifteen-minute trade lag time, meaning that traders couldn't get access to the newest and latest market information. It created a blind spot that caused massive causalities and money lost.

Sometimes cyber attackers will start a train of happenings that will indirectly affect your for months at a time. Other times, they will simply target out your wallet, mining pool, or even your computer. Make sure you have all of the available security and you constantly keep your eyes on your funds and the rises and falls of the market.

Bitcoin is doing all they can in order to stop the attacks, but it isn't possible to reign everyone in. From hackers to men living in their parent's basements, everyone who wants to make a quick buck is going to try as hard as they can to make it a reality. Stay vigilant.

Psychology and Timing

While you can't track the rises and falls of the Bitcoin market quite like you can with the regular stock market, there are ways to use psychology to make educated guesses or hypoteses about what the market is going to do. It is best to make notes about the following when you are looking to do some trading.

Days of the Week: What days of the week see more movement? Make sure you mark it down – Fridays might be a little busier because people aren't paying as much attention at work, whereas Mondays will be a little slower because people are still quite groggy from the weekend and the start of the workweek.

Time of Day: Forgetting just the day, consider monitoring the time of day. Are people buying and selling more during the morning of the afternoon? What about after the workday ends? Lunch hour? By making note of these important times, you will be able to schedule yourself time to pay extra attention. You can use busier times to your advantage, but you can also definitely use those slower times as well. Don't take just a week as the gospel truth, instead monitor it over a few weeks.

Holidays: Are the markets faster or slower during the holidays? Typically from November through December, people are taking money out of Bitcoins in order to purchase presents and trips back to their hometowns. Pay special attention to the market during that time. Once the New Year starts up again, then more and more people will be coming back into the market. You should also consider paying attention during tax season, at the start of the summer, and in August and September for the start of the school year.

Events: Make sure you pay attention to daily events that can happen on Bitcoin. The Toyko based Mt. Gox went down for an hour in 2013 after the value of the currency rose 20%, this had a massive, massive impact on the relative value of the Bitcoin. Make sure to pay attention to things like weather events as well – if the entire East Coast of the United States is going to have an ice storm that will knock out power for a week or even just a few days, people are going to pull their money out, and quickly.

The way you track any of this information is up to you. You can make a legal pad full of notes that you follow, or you can track it in an Excel sheet. The important part is that you are constantly watching and making notes that you understand. Once again, this is where it would be a great idea to have a team of people working together to help each other out.

SUCCESS (AND CAUTIONARY) STORIES

If you are feeling hesitant about starting to buy and trade Bitcoins, here are just a few success stories to get you motivated.

Norway

A man named Kristoffer Koch decided, on a complete whim, that he was going to invest $150 kroner (which is about $26 dollars in the United States) in Bitcoin in 2009. That simple $26 (what many people spend on coffee in a typical week), lead to a return investment of $850,000 or roughly 158,978 cups of coffee. Koch did not know much about the currency, but was doing research for his thesis on encryption and decided to put a small investment into the Bitcoin out of curiosity. He had no idea what he did was give himself a sizeable next egg for the future. What did he do next? He forgot about it.

He forgot about the $26 and continued on with his life, graduated college, got a job, and started a family. It was not until the media and his friends started discussing the Bitcoin attention that he even remembered that small amount of money. His curiosity piqued, he had to think long and hard about his password to his wallet. It took him a few months, but he figured it out.

"It said I had 5,000 bitcoins in there. Measuring that in today's rates it's about five million kroner," Koch told NRK, according to a Guardian translation. 5,000 Bitcoins is $850,000.

Had he waited until today, his initial investment, with the single Bitcoin being worth $210, would be worth approximately $1 million cold hard cash.

18

Koch isn't the only person who has benefitted from the rise in bitcoins' worth and popularity. According to an April report by Bloomberg Businessweek, the success of the world's first decentralized, peer-to-peer digital currency has spawned many overnight millionaires.

Younger Generations

But Bitcoin doesn't only belong to those who have a college education. A well-timed investment of $1,000 in gift money by a 15 year old boy from Idaho has allowed him to earn 110x that money ($110,000) and start his own education startup.

Erik Finman took $1,000 he received as an Easter gift from his grandmother and invested it in Bitcoin back in 2012, according to a report by Mashable. After holding steady in Bitcoin for over a year, Finman sold his bitcoins for $110,000 – making him one of the youngest success stories out there.

Luckily for Finman, he sold his stash of bitcoins when the price hovered around $1,200 per bitcoin.

Finman, in the long run, decided to reinvest his earnings into Botangle.com, an online video tutoring service that "allows students and tutors access to a diverse array of resources that just do not exist in a normal classroom setting," according to its official website. Most notably of his success and company, Finman pays his employees in Bitcoin. He told Mashable that he enjoys "sharing the wealth of bitcoin", saying:

"I have no doubt it will be huger [sic] than anyone can imagine right now. Bitcoin is like the Internet in the '90s."

During a question-and-answer session that he took part in after his success on an Entrepreneur subreddit, Finman explained how he first came to learn about bitcoin, writing:

"I owe a lot to my older brother. He told me about bitcoins and help[ed] me get set up with 0.2 bitcoins that he gave me. And my grandmother just out of the blue gave me a $1,000 check for Easter."

He continued by saying that he accrued more Bitcoins and planned on making even more, "So that I can trump my brother in how many bitcoins he had," adding that he first learned about Bitcoin in 2010.

Though entrepreneurs today may not be able to replicate Finman's success, or they may fear doing so due to the risks and busier market, they can learn from those who have entered the industry through more conventional in-roads.

Cautionary Tale

Finally, we have a cautionary tale to keep in mind when setting up your Bitcoin account.

A male Bitcoin trader tells his tale occasionally, never revealing his name or location. In May of 2011, he put in $75 into Bitcoin. He played around for a few weeks and then went through one of the biggest crashes in Bitcoin history. After that, he lost interest, thinking he would never be able to recoup his money.

He stopped playing and moved onto something else.

When Bitcoin introduced encryptable wallets, he set up an impenetrable password. That little bit got him interested again, and he started buying a selling again, sending money to that locked wallet. Once the prices started rising again, he wanted to take his money and run. Just one problem: he didn't remember that impenetrable password that he had set up.

What does he know? He knows that he wrote down the password in a notebook that is somewhere in his house – possible in a notebook with all of his school things that just so happens to be the attic. He does not remember his password, and he's not sure he'll think of it in time.

For now, he's hoping that he can find the notebook and unlock his wallet. He knows he's still earning money and has a nice little fun set up for him. Bitcoin cannot access his password either.

Make sure you know where you put your wallet password, or you will have a ton of (possibly inaccessible) money just sitting in cyberspace.

CONCLUSION

There is no doubt that investing in the Bitcoin can be profitable. There is also no doubt that investing in the Bitcoin can be extremely dangerous. This is not one of those "get rich quickly" schemes, and this is not a cheat to get out of working for your money. In fact, to make the money you would need to survive, you'd have to work really, really hard.

Weigh the pros and cons, and talk to people on message boards or in forums that can educate you on what they have gone through. There are a plethora of YouTube videos out there that will help you along your path, including interviews with successes and failures. Though it may seem like pretend because it is on the internet, Bitcoins can cost you real money.

The best advice to take is to start very small. Do not go all in unless you know what you are doing, you know how to play the game, and you know you will get money out at the other end, no matter how long it takes you to get there.

Still, you can't be too cautious. You are not going to get anywhere unless you start. It's much like learning how to use a new phone or how to drive a car, eventually you will get better at reading the signs and you'll know where to click, who to talk to, and what moves to make.

I want to personally Thank You for reading this book! I sincerely hope the information contained will help you to understand the basics of the digital currency of the future: Bitcoins. In an ever-evolving global economy, it's easy to see the benefits of this crypto-currency, while also recognizing the possible pitfalls. The best idea is to keep yourself abreast of the information, and staying well-informed of the technology and logistics behind this game-changing digital currency of the future.

Finally, if you enjoyed this book, please take the time to share your thoughts and post a positive review on Amazon. I would greatly appreciate your support!

Thank you and good luck!

Benjamin Tideas

BONUS FREE RESOURCES accompanying this book at
www.plaid-enterprises.com/bitcoin

Get my kindle books for FREE! Visit www.plaid-enterprises.com